FRETWORK

POEMS

LYNNE THOMPSON

MARSH HAWK PRESS ~ 2019

ISBN: 978–0–996–99115–5

First Edition 10 9 8 7 6 5 4 3

Marsh Hawk Press books are published by Marsh Hawk Press, Inc.,
a not-for-profit corporation under section 501 (c) 3 United States Internal Revenue Code.

Cover art "Coup de Grâce" by Alison Saar
Author photo on cover by Jacqueline Legazcue

Book design by Heather Wood
www.heatherwoodbooks.com

The text is set in Berkeley Oldstyle Book.

Library of Congress Cataloging-in-Publication Data
Thompson, Lynne, 1951– author
Fretwork / Lynne Thompson
First edition | East Rockaway: Marsh Hawk Press, 2019
LCCN 2018035327 | ISBN 9780996991155
LCC PS3620.H6836 A6 2019 | DDC 811/.6—dc23
LC record available at https://lccn.loc.gov/2018035327

Marsh Hawk Press
P.O. Box 206, East Rockaway, NY 11518-0206
www.marshhawkpress.org

This book is dedicated
to my nieces and nephews and cousins
and to their children and theirs....

Contents

We have no solace but utterance,
hence this wild cry.

—DEREK WALCOTT

Composition #1

If I say the woman who birthed me betrayed me,
you may think that woman badly distilled, needful.

But if I say she who betrayed me was herself betrayed,
you may think of the woman as gesture, exile, spilled out,

because when we think of exile or the innocent gesture—
if there's any such thing as a gesture that's innocent—

we should also think intolerable mirror, the mirror never
reflecting that it could become obsession or that it might,

perhaps, just peel away. If I say peel or blunder or mercy,
you might think my vision too fragile and you're half-right:

from somewhere, unbidden, the woman waylaid by my birth
whistles: *here's a swaying bridge, cross over, compose the dark.*

Beverly Meets My Father

In her upswept hair, suspicion,
while he holds a cracked cup
over sweet eucalyptus, a-flame.

The circus arrives and every
clown is arrested on the spot.
Rain falls until it can no longer.

The fire breather is excellent.

While She Was Out Stealing, I Slept in Beverly's Womb

but it was dark and I did not go far.
She smelled the way the Taj Mahal smells by moonlight.
Minutes went by on tiptoe with their fingers to their lips.

Then her hands dropped and jerked at something
and the robe she was wearing came open—
but it was dark and I did not go far.

She was thinking and it was clear—even on short acquaintance—
thinking was always going to be a bother to her.
Minutes went by on tiptoe with their fingers to their lips.

From thirty feet away, she looked like a lot of class—
enough woman to make a priest discard his vestments—
but it was dark and I did not go far.

She smiled a smile I felt in my hip pocket. She made me
a pawn to her indifference then.
But it was dark and I did not go far.
Minutes went by on tiptoe with their fingers to their lips.

Wombsong

Here I am, mom—all motive and
gristle and moaning for a daddy
but that bell just won't ring. What

a playpen you were: Isle of Langerhans,
echo of Charlie Parker, miasma of
hominy, chayote, and fried fat-back.

No call to worry, my maker of mysteries.
You took a gamble, gave me away, and
neither of us will ever know all it cost.

Petition

Some of it, of course, is true. The day, month, year
of my birth—all is true. Two years later, timing
stopped on a dime. A "Certificate of Live Birth" is

issued—is almost all untrue never mind the autograph
of County General's attending physician who's never
been heard from again. My weight in the record? Well,

was anyone ever such a lock to pry? Female, yes. But
my new parents—*Caribbeans-Who've-Come-Lately?*—
finally true when they filed their Petition to Adopt,

Case Number *Anno Domini* _____, seeking custody of
me, the minor, Pamela Marie. True: petitioners lived in
the County of Los Angeles; true, petitioners were more

than 10 years older than the minor; true, the minor was born
(see above) and the new parents, having consented in court
and signed all the papers (blah and more legal blah) hereby

& henceforth would, in all cases, respect and treat the minor
as their child and the child would sustain toward them a legal
relationship and have all rights and be subject to all the duties

(never fully specified) of that relationship and would forever-
more be known as *Little Girl T*____ and be sent to live with
petitioners. As for Pamela Marie? Never heard from again.

Terrible Fortune Inside My Head, Grenadine

inspired by Alison Saar's sculpture "Foundered"

...and my head lies, eternally, on its side, its
one unbound ear cocked to the wind (always
howling, racing away, exposed, expectant)

...and though my head is made of glass, nothing
could be less clear, caked with the dark world's
detritus: bone, tissue, links of chain, centuries

...and if my head is made of glass, it could not
be more clear-cut if only you would look closely:
above my throat, behind both occluded eyes

...if you look, you'll see the ship—its masts time-
worn, ragged—routes unremembered—(could it
be the unnamed slaver that ran aground at Spring?)

...and though my ancestors cannot tell me if its
provenance—its terrible fortune—is false or true,
the ship moans, unmoored, for all that's been lost

...my head sideways to history, my free ear tintin-
abulating old miseries of a terror that scored walls
in Elmina Castle & all the tortured shrieking inside...

Trace

To unearth what came before, ask
    how did they come?   when?

        *

About one hundred years before Daddy
left Barbados for New York, the schooner

        Irene arrived in Havana,
1822, guns mounted. Two hundred eighty-

eight of the three hundred thirty-one free
people put on board at Bonny disembarked

sold as slaves   *run*   *run*

        *

Of his surname—*Thompson*—think: former
owner
    last owner   names
           lost   *run away*

official records (State & church)   *run*

baptism   marriage   oral history   maps
   registers   masks

  run   wills & archives

    run away   *away*

slave complaints, debts, laws (former slaves
    as owners of slaves)
                    RUN

      auctions   *away*

          *

        They entered here

Emigrations

A girl put her hand into the pocket
of her mother's lap—believed her
mother would stay with her forever

in this bewildering nation until her
mother no longer stayed—only the girl
remained—cold hands, no pockets.

*

Friendless aboard the vessel *Van Dyck,*
his Bible clutched under his arm, a young

man waved to each dark & lovely who had
prized him because he relied on the Book:

thou shall be removed into
                    all kingdoms of the earth

Genesis

I

…on twenty-seven March, 1899, Dora rose from her pallet,
came to squat, and my father flopped out like a fish. One
month later, American Negroes fasted in protest of the lynch
laws, but Daddy, born to *got nothing* in a British colony, took
off nonetheless and despite everything…

> *all gurgle and shit,*
> *a wheel, turning, his eyes fixed,*
> *history nascent…'*

II

"I left that floating hotel, the *Van Dyck*, to arrive—via Barbados—
on the Isle of Tears, June, 1923, and I didn't care what. We'd
heard the news back home about a black man, Sam Hose, lynched
for killing his Georgia white employer. Hose was burned alive,
knuckles put up for sale and *that'll teach* `em at the local grocer's,
but I came anyway…"

> *The journey of not*
> *knowing isn't bitter or*
> *a sweet seed, just chance…*

"…I came for four years to earn money teaching grammar and
numerals the way I taught grammar and numerals to youngsters
back home, knowing few black boys in the States were allowed
to attend school, not knowing if any school would hire me…"

The twins, color and cry,
steal each other's breath, yet they
grow under heaven.

"I came despite the rebellions: the Robert Charles Riots, 1900,
28 dead; the Wilmington Insurrection, no official death count;
Springfield, 1908; Houston, 1917; District of Columbia, 1919;
and all the unnamed revolutions every year since and in between."

Time's a magician—
sleight of hand and a white mask—
black fingers, unbound.

III

"When I said *I will come back,* Dora shook her head and sobbed.
I came anyway."

The Van Dyck

…was recommissioned for His Majesty's Service in 1939 and
deployed to evacuate Narvik, its Allied Forces and a few Jews,

June, 1940, until she ran afoul of Nazi torpedos. But that's the end
of her story. It began when the *Van Dyck* was built after the war

to end all of them. She launched February, 1921, full throttle for
Montevideo, Pernambuco, Barbados, New York. Fortnightly services

she gave to the *hoi polloi* and a fine lot of them came aboard: Anna
Pavlova and her *corps de ballet* bedazzled on the main deck, while

Shackleton, the Arctic explorer, was sailing his last spring-tide topside,
his rheumy eyes watching the passing as he leaned out from her stern.

Still, lower decks for lesser classes were the best places for hi-jinx and
hard tack. This is their history, too. Ellis Island's log books tell tales

of the Portuguese, Chinese, Italians, and Caribbean Brits. Of the Silvas
and Paynes who came to Brooklyn but not until every alien answered:

who paid for your passage? How much money are you bringing?
Are you deformed—a polygamist—an anarchist? Each was examined.

In 1923, A.R. Jenkins, M.D., inspected young schoolmaster Thompson
who came—like many others—crossing after crossing—coveting America's

"normalcy." A Grenadine, young Thompson, my daddy, my ole man,
history's onlooker, a witness to how it all dissolves into watery graves…

Suspended

Not only the scale—Chrysler, Flatiron,
     Empire State—all of which,
          he realized, would

tower over the tamarind and huckleberry
     beloved in his Antilles.
          Not the Lazarus-hailed statue

guarding the harbor he sailed into or
     Harlem's rent parties or
          the double-decked, suspended

Verrazano Bridge connecting the islands
     at the Narrows, or Sugar Hill, or
          the storefront churches; not even

Claude McKay's *If We Must Die*. No. What shackled
     Daddy's breath was the men he approached,
          men with skin dark rum like his, common

men who worked the Grand Central. An innocent, Daddy asked
     will the Brooklyn train depart within the hour? These
          Americans replied: *you sho' talk funny   for a nigger*

In America's Mirror

Neither bridge nor trapeze.
Neither absence nor plot.

Just a hobo with the scent of a scavenger,
the romanticized stink of a jackal as in

Darfur, Port-au-Prince, or New York City—

(bullet-riddled skull there,
neat cough,
helix, calcium)—

but neither tundra nor cobblestone.

Neither sharecropper nor fireworks nor pillar,
                          just a callous brunette
                          gerrymandering the night.

Flotsam. Labyrinth.
Unkempt ambition.
Ashes on the shallow moon.

A little too dangerous.
A little thistle.

All longitude and moonshine.

But neither smoke nor spinet, neither blue-
stem nor stammer in the white mayhem.

Bout for Jack & a West Indian Immigrant

The year Mother arrived on Ellis Island, the heavyweight fighter,
Jack Johnson, began serving a one-year sentence in Leavenworth
for violating the Mann Act, but everybody knew

Jack was doing time for loving a whole lot of white women,
and each and every one of them every which-way.
Mother, fresh from hibiscus and the Caribbean Sea,

knew nothing of it; didn't know that some who thought
if you're light, well alright, would look at her and wonder
is she a white girl...?

I never asked about color when I could have; never thought of
the past as prologue because in the Civil Rights-free-sex-60s,
black was a beauty

and I didn't want to think about the pale man who had
bedded my Grannie; that my own Mother was grey pearl,
chipped tooth, the other white meat...

Lift

It was magic, Mother said when asked.
Your Gran & my auntie & I walked into
a room with people we did not know.
No one closed the doors but the doors
closed and the room flew up and up,
then the doors came open and we all
walked out, wonder stilling her voice.

Inter-mix'd

Although he chose to lie with another
and turned absent father because of it,

Daddy hitched his fate to Mother.
Mother was fair in complexion (one clue

being her name—cobbled together from Low
German, Middle Dutch, some Old English:

hesel, hasil, hasel, hazel) but even that
hegemony didn't deter him, proud as he was

of his Igbo; proud he faced windward after
the Bight of Biafra/Bight of Bonny; pleased

to feed his family cassava & taro root. In a time
when many thought he would not have been,

he was learnéd. When he looked at her, when
she spoke her name, he might have thought

*Let the Angler fit himself with a Hazle of one piece
or two set conveniently together* (Cox, 1677)

or *the note of hasel springeth* (Hazlitt, 1864).
He might have thought of her as his hazel-wand or

hazel-hooped or a dervish of hazel-wizard healing
his scarifications, her body fully salt-fish & chickpea.

What he thought is lost to time but never can be.
He anointed himself with oil of hazel: see his

children sitting, as Virgil said, *beneath the grateful*
shade which hazles, intermix'd with elms, have made?

Carnival

I

Forget the birth thing.
Forget about her:

> she was a beauty
> or she wasn't.
> She spoke softly

> or laughed like a man
> who slugs five fingers
> of whiskey every day.

> She loved a carnival
> (but only when it came to town.)

> She had a hunger
> for the short, short story

> and asked for everything
> that happened, then put it
> behind her as soon as.

Forget this irrelevant history.
Can anyone know what is true?

II

Forget the planet is spinning so hard
you can't call it anything but memory.

You've already forgotten first memories
(how they half-skip, won't speak)

& you've already forgotten your father:

>maybe he was a rogue or believed
>in holy, holy, but no matter.

>Every day he was,
>he wasn't. A blessing.

III

Forget you slipped beyond
your mother's wide hips
after waiting to forget:

the hugger-mugger of the coming through,
the Sisters forgetting to cross their foreheads.
Forget the insignificant chance, the burr.

Be of rare cheer and don't be fooled.
The carnival lasts only minutes.
Don't forget your mask.

Overnight Bag, Blue, with Broken Handle

Mother's old overnight has half a handle
held in place with a rusty safety pin and
the scent of where that bag has been
still clings to the silk several decades on.
A corroded pin clasps family stories:
her four boys' grade cards;
photographs, of course, some with
no label and well-past recognition;
immigration papers—her's, her husband's.
Hidden behind the bag's topstitching,
securing a mirror too speckled to give off
a proper reflection, a transit stub
for the *City of New Orleans*, the train bound
from Chicago to the Big Easy on a spring day,
1929, speeding south as the darker race ran north.

She had not run, exactly,
because she knew (inexactly) who she was.
She may have squirmed in an unyielding seat
and eyed her baby with a sigh,
her baby being the only reason
she couldn't lounge in the *whites only* club car.
None of that mattered. She was on her way
to the land of filé and jambalaya, of King Creole
and Saturday nights that lasted well past Sundays,
nights when she black-bottomed in Congo Square.
She would leave her son with a neighbor
then let the neighbor's son stroke her
cheek and throat with jasmine petals.
She'd forget about her husband and south-side
Chicago. Of course, she could not stay.

Another Migration

Daddy Vincentian come lately to Chicago and, of course,
developed a *bad* pneumonia, the croup filling the lungs of
a man wrecked young by asthma. *A drier climate,* some
doctor suggested, looking out of his window for a pacific.

In 1930, Daddy Drove to California Without Benefit of "The Negro Traveler's Green Book"

I

Daddy left Chicago with Mr. Rodriguez instead
of his wife, planning to travel Route 66, having
little to less money, and eager to see the Pacific.

When he wanted to sleep, it would have helped
if he'd known Mrs. Mosby's "tourist home," 1614
Jackson, Springfield, welcomed weary Negroes.

If he needed gas in Tulsa, Oklahoma, *Swindalls*
would have been the station for his kind. For a bite
to eat in Amarillo, he would have been given a tip:

"try Tom's Place, New Harlem, or Blue Bonnet" and
so on across the country. He had no guide; had only
the risk of a rope in Oklahoma City or Santa Fe, N.M.

Because they were driving to California, the Golden
State, maybe they didn't know many towns within
its borders were "sundowners" and there, "Ain't No

Niggers Allowed" was the policy. They were headed
to the City of Angels but in others: Burbank, Compton,
Culver City, Dutch Flat, Gold Run, Downey, Folsom,

Lynwood, Inglewood, Orange, Palmdale, and the San
Fernando Valley, they could not eat or sleep. Yet to
make the news: Siskiyou County's last lynching, 1935.

II

With the introduction of this travel guide in 1936,
it has been our idea to give the Negro traveler
information that will keep him from running

into difficulties and embarrassments, and to make
his trip more enjoyable. There will be a day—
despite the introduction of this travel guide—

sometime in the near future when it will not
have to be published. That is when there will be
an end to days of difficulties and embarrassments,

when we as a race will have equal opportunities
and privileges in these United States. We trust
sometime in the near future, there'll be the great

day when we'll be able to suspend publication
for then we'll be able to go wherever we please,
when we as a race will have equal opportunities

and no embarrassments. But until that day comes,
we shall continue to distribute this information,
this travel guide Mr. Green introduced in 1936,
critical directions that kept Negroes from running...

III

It was 1966 before *The Green Book* printed its last.

Virgil Avenue & Other Geographies

I

It was a beginning like any other which isn't
 quite the way it was. With beginnings,

where to start? The house that was my first
 was a house that Daddy brought to Virgil

atop a flatbed truck. He made his boys fix
 it to the foundation, then do what ever else

was needed to create a kind of permanence.
 I wasn't there then. Then I was, driving Daddy

through the old neighborhood where the house was,
 as memories tend to be, smaller than he remembered.

II

I was part of his vision of a wind-whipped Schwinn, part get-away, part
stay-put, all pout and tough rules, *Dragnet* and *Jack Benny*. But I had a
mind, and I began to pursue the life of it. Only half-present, only vaguely
aware of something beyond presence. Of those years, I recall a boy—
Henry—not as I knew him then, but the way I knew him when I was never
to see him again, realizing too late his Armenian surname had been thrown
on a heap. You might ask why he never told me. You might ask why everyone
is always looking behind; perhaps

III

...because it is all ephemeral by which I mean to say
every one of us gets suckered by the gods. California,

for example, the first of the fifty states to honor an insect—
a Dogface butterfly with a glide-range that can't

outspread the topography's shifting, golden borders—
it's bluish-black, sulfur-yellow insufficient to hoodwink

permanence with its showy display in the chaparral of the
southern Santa Anas. Tribe: *coliadini;* genus: *z. Eurydice.*

The Dresser

When she told me Kay Francis died with no one
beside her bed, I understood Mother remembered
dressing that silver screen star—that she'd worked

unseen in the trailer, a safe distance from the gems
and furbelows, *yes ma'am*ing while Francis stood,
insisted: "A little shorter—no, a little longer—oh,

can't you highlight the shadows above my breasts?"
Mother slaved early mornings into late evenings;
glad for it because money was tight, food scarce, so

scarce she hoped no one saw the scraps she smuggled
from the studio's buffet, hoping the bits wouldn't spoil
before she boarded the trolley, finally, fingers cramping,

knees throbbing from kneeling on straight pins and one
thousand colored bugle beads. Of course she remembered
as she warned: *in the end, we are all just women, alone—*

Hammer & Pick

Long before I came along

a dream

Daddy told his boys he was glad
for any kind of work and FDR
with his New Deal politics was his guy

always there

If it wasn't for the WPA, my brothers say,
they would have had nothing to eat

peace and glory

Daddy's talent to draw a bow across a fiddle
wouldn't keep a roof over their heads,
and he was happy to go down to the sewers

instead of waiting

glad to slip below the earth before sun-
rise, to return to it in starlight

Undeterred,   *built a railroad*

swung the hammer & pick, the other men
twice his size, strength, but Daddy did
whatever he was told

now he's done

He wasn't thinking of history
only hoped his boys would survive
another potatoes-and-water supper

don't you remember

The brothers say they were better off
than many. They were the ones with a drum.

Doomsday Haiku

Shame it's not Ornette
Coleman. You're hearing the earth
screaming, the doomed birds.

Magnet

I have to see a thing a thousand
times before I see it once.
—Thomas Wolfe

My parents never read Thomas Wolfe so
when they went to the isles again, reasons
varied: he had promised, and she had
married him and the promises she had

no way of knowing. It wouldn't last.
There, he would be the radio expert
he had taught himself to be. She
would watch over their two sons when

she wasn't enjoying a certain notoriety.
My brothers were going to learn to love
the Caribbean but work was just as hard
to find as in California and Daddy had

only one radio to fix. *Took it apart then*
put it back together more times than I
could count, Mother's tone turned dry.
She was pregnant with her third when

they rushed to return to the States, when
she learned that her family could return
but, with no papers, she could not. How
she did, only coins in greedy palms know.

Émigré

Maybe it was reflex. Maybe it was memory and want—want for
  the scent of soursop and sugar apples, memory of the flight of

a frigate bird, that made us drive every Sunday, down Vine Street,
  past Forest Lawn Cemetery, to Griffith Park, where Daddy, nutmeg-

colored and clad head-to-toe in his all-whites, came to play cricket
  and make believe he was home in Buccament Valley, St. Vincent,

West Indies, where he could be the man home would have made
  of him although none of that meant one EC dollar to me because

in those days, cricket—with its ball of string & hard cork, wooden
  stumps & willow-carved-blades-turned-into-bats—was an odd British

formality, a long-ago when ladies wore pale hose and organdy hats and
  I was allowed to wear my Sunday finery (as long as I didn't grass-

stain my not-for-school skirt), drink tea in Royal Crown cups, and wolf
  down cucumber-and-cream-cheese sandwiches those old world women

made for their men to devour during the break in the game, which
  might last for a leisurely hour or more, before the teams would

take up again in a throe of fear because Daddy was the game's best
  bowler, and with his elbow cocked, and a lightning rotation of his

arm, he threw googlies, leg-breaks, and flippers; always got his man
  and took the wicket because Daddy could bring the heat—although

he never would have said *bring the heat* because his home rule kind of
schooling favored the King's English over the colloquial. But it was

exactly this heat-bringing and resplendent use of language that made
him the kind of man to be reckoned with, and I worked hard to grasp it.

The Downfall of Mankind

Erasers on pencils
Women wearing hair curlers outdoors
Failure to enunciate
Careless thinking
No thinking
Failure to wear a tie
Failure to wear a jacket
Profanity (except for him)
A lack of chocolate & Scotch whiskey
Doctors (unless they are relatives)
Wasted energy
Wasted time
Waste
Erasers
Failure to love:

       westerns (*Bonanza*)
       roller derby
       Shakespeare

Rock-and-roll
Failure to remember
Wars
Lack of ambition
Poor handwriting
Lack of direction
Lawyers (unless they are relatives)
Lack of attention
Lack of curiosity
Houses set too close to the street
Politicians (especially when they are relatives)

Inattentive nurses
Erasers,

Daddy said.

Iron Horses & the Moon

Late as '56, Mother warned: "watch out for hoboes" recalling
the year she followed her husband to California; that no-so-long-

ago of Jim Crow and the Great Depression; the same year many
thousands of lost-my-home Okies fled the Dust Bowl, "those

dirty sons of bitches." Entertainment linked us. In 1935, movie
houses proclaimed "Negroes & Okies upstairs" because everyone

knew Okies were lazy, shiftless and sometimes, incested their own.
"Hungry and likely to do anything `cause of it," the courts agreed:

"convicts, paupers, idiots and lunatics, as well as persons likely
to become a public charge" were driven from the Golden State's

borders. Alarmed my favorite playground wasn't too far from
the tracks of the Southern Pacific's iron horses, Mother sneered:

"that's where they congregate and they love an easy mark." She
never betrayed the times she'd pocketed less than a nickel-note.

She never suspected that I'd already been on the fly until the day
I declared "I'd like to ride a cannonball possum-belly, be a road kid

with a stake." Daddy didn't look up, said he'd helped many a hitcher,
given them a buck or ride to a motel just one step above a flop house.

"You're the worst kind of sucker," Mother mocked. But me and my
Daddy?—we just wanted to run; to sleep beneath a California moon.

Fretwork

By the time Mother took me to her birthplace—Bequia—
I was a fifth-grade wordsmith in a first-grader's body.
H-o-m-e—too easy—fell off my spelling list although

I didn't know what home meant. I didn't recognize my
Mother's mother who was the color of pitch and whether
she was pleased to see her daughter and me, she kept it

to herself, a mystery. "Tonight" Mother said, "we'll sleep
under cotton netting to keep the mosquitoes from eating
us up" and, like that of the man who delivered his catch

in the early light, her voice echoed. Later, as Gran's house
went dark, a bauble of moon glistening off the fretwork,
Mother found me atop a chest of drawers—(I knew how

to save myself, opened each drawer, more, and then more,
then scaled each one, musty with a scent of lies and Hazell
history)—shivering in the night's damp air. When she asked,

I said I was hiding from the mosquitoes. When I saw my first,
on a screen, I frowned. "How do they *eat you up?*" "Nothing's
as you imagine it," Mother said, and she wasn't speaking to me.

Haiku—more or less—
for West Indian Palates

Curried goat, curried
goat spice, sauté & simmer,
to dinner sit ye down.

Guinea corn, sorghum,
rub ye teeth to make `em
clean, sorghum, guinea corn.

Curry blend, cumin,
allspice, paprika and
dark, dark honey.

Filé powder from
the Gulf Coast. Dried,
ground, put in de gumbo.

Stamp-and-go, salt cod cakes
take me down to Kingstown,
take me back to home.

Mashed bananas, see ye
Gibbons Bay. Cook a fiery
stew, serve hot, sweet.

Plantain—do not peel.
Cut half-wise. Brush
with oil. Grill or broil.

Six pigs' ears, six small
rolls. Mustard ye cabbage.
Spicy sauce. Serve at once.

Lost Spirits

Daddy was laughing but he sat quite still
the day he told us what he had seen:
an Obeah man with one eye, smiling.

Daddy, young, played alone, as he often
did, or with boys from the next plantation.
He was laughing but sat quite still, his

eyes unlocked as he remembered racing
up the hill he was forbidden until he came
upon the Obeah man with one eye, smiling.

We loved his stories of *Papa Bois,* of *douens*
with backward-facing feet, of ancient whimsy
because he was laughing while sitting so still

and looking beyond a great distance, knowing
between *Papa Bois* and death is a connection
to the Obeah man with one eye, smiling, but

he just looked at us then winked his left, said
I ran away before anything wicked happened.
Again he laughed but sat so still as he spoke
to us of an Obeah man with one eye, smiling.

Queens

conjure man spits out pieces of glass,
pins, needles, snails, shells, vials, lizards,
spiders, flies, cat's teeth, snakeskins
and fragments of bone
                                    —Gerald Hausman & Ray Griffin

Mother & her sister were always
proper, proper, proper and told
they were descended from queens.
Black queens and white queens.
Nefertiti and Victoria
telling their daughters & theirs:

> *here's your scepter, baby;*
> *stroll that red carpet but*
> *watch out for the rip…*

Watch out. Behind the door.
Obeah-man got a secret
and it ain't about no queens.
He say: *remember ya auntie?*
The last queen before the queen
that was your mother? The last proper,
her legs crossed just above her ankles?
She bought your throne. Bought it
with her strong black thighs.
Bought it from the church parading
in the body of a pale Scot minister.
Your auntie, she say: "lie down
on me bed, Father; lie down.
Curry this callaloo, pepperpot,

allspice, all the time. Crown me,
sweet Jesus. Answer me prayers."

And you that come after? Queens,
baby, and proper, proper, proper.

Antilles, lesser

When you're a girl and your Daddy tells you
he was born in the lesser Antilles, you don't ask
questions. Truth is, you don't really know what

Antilles are, barely know lesser although you do
know about comparisons. You have book smarts:
have read the oeuvre of Dumas *pére* & Dumas *fils,*

read about Alexander the Great (which suggests
there must have been an Alexander the Less but
you've never read anything about him and can

just imagine how embarrassed his kinfolk must be.)
Anyway, when Daddy tells you about these lesser
Antilles, these small islands, you worry they're just

magic dust and they are because when you go to look
on a map, mid-20th century, those islands aren't there
which is humiliating because then you go to school

where some little white girls are boasting of County
Cork or about a Seder their forefathers prepared in
what's now called Prague—easy to find on McNally's—

& all you can say is: "my people were born in the West
Indies, Antilles" (trying much too hard to sound exotic.)
But Mrs. Lordamore's exacting, wants to know "where

in the Antilles?" while she goes on to tell the class how
Cristóbal Colon (aka Columbus) landed there when he
wasn't looking for America; specifically, that he landed

in the Bahamas and then she turns to you, asks "are you saying *your* people come from the Bahamas?" And you pucker your forehead the way you do when you want

others to think you need time to remember but you're already remembering your Daddy looking glassy-eyed when he sermonized about the Antilles, about plantain

and rum. But just now, Mrs. Lordamore's still waiting, saying "show us, show us on the map" and now you can barely stand and when you do, you walk very s-l-o-w-l-y

to the map, point to the place you already know isn't there and pray and glory hallelujah!—prayers do get answered— the school bell rings and it's the last day before Christmas

vacation and you're sure everyone, even Mrs. Lordamore, will forget the question by the time you all return, January next. And all of them do. But I didn't forget although

it was years before I saw Daddy's St. Vincent (his lesser island) on a map. And by then, Daddy didn't talk about sweet fruit anymore. It's left to me to find anyone to tell.

Telling

Maybe
he never knew—

maybe he fucked you
like you were a planet

who made his life turn
uncommon for a while—

Did you go back to him
more than once or maybe

he never knew you
again? Perhaps

there were paper kites
and some laughter but

what did that have to do
with either of you?

Maybe he was impeccable
or a lapsed Catholic given

to mesmerism and cocaine.
Maybe he forgot to bring you

camellias. But Beverly, did
you ever tell him about me?

Danse Macabre

The first time I left was the last.
I was little more than a seed then
& my birth father wasn't innocent.
Perhaps he didn't even notice?

I was little more than a seed then
swimming in the Fallopian Sea and
who knows whether he noticed
his woman's tears already forming.

I was swimming in Fallopian Seas,
was more than a little complicit
in the making of Beverly's tears,
the distance growing between us.

I have been more than complicit,
neglecting to seek him out, a distance
between us eternally growing,
this far-and-wide our common bond.

I've neglected to go out and find him,
have written so many ridiculous myths,
estrangement our common bond,
the distance growing by turns, twists.

Wherever you're reading this, know:
none of us are innocent. We all—
all-knowing—fail to go in search of.
The first time I left wasn't the last.

Ambition

He'd longed to savor the rivers of the Grenadines
in his mouth—another taste of Fancy, taste of moss
and green lizard—to smell the balm of honeybees

(*apis mellifera*) in their rookery of parallel combs.
But two mad boys, much too ambitious to be men,
set upon my father as he entered the night school's

john. These rowdies battered him on the most complex
curve of his head, then made off with his children's
allowance. This attack on a part-time teacher didn't

make the ten o'clock news and Daddy's hospital stay
was brief. When he came home, Mother prepared
his favorites: roast lamb with red potatoes & thyme,

almond-dressed green beans, sweet cakes purled with
lemon. And leftover? All he would never again taste
or smell. He ate nothing but air at all our meals, after.

Mother Taught Me Ugly—

for Christine & Satchi

every summer morning
when she'd wake us up and
untangle our slim brown legs
nightly knitted into coverlets
while we slept
under covers of dark.
Yawning, we'd stumble-fall
into the bathroom, share
shower, half-brush teeth,
scramble for scrambled eggs
and bacon, dress uniformly:
shorts, T-shirts, open-toe sandals,
then march in to her for the Rite
of Braiding Little Girls' Hair.

Mother always began the ceremony
with them, one after the other,
then visa versa,
every other day.
The one with green eyes
had one thousand loose, soft curls
and took more time but
Mother didn't mind & always sang
steal away
for the first forty minutes
brushing then ending
by binding the two butt-long braids

together at their bottoms
with tri-colored ribbons
kept in an old cigarette box.

After, you could still see
the chaotic ringlets burst
merrily from those braids,

flapping about like the tails
of friendly mermaids.

The other one had dark eyes,
black as Chinese pools
where monks are said
to mine for secrets.
She had no curls
but Mother didn't mind,
just worked rhythmically
for sixty minutes to weave waves
into arrow-straight hair,
then tied it
with white silk threads,
whistling softly to herself
while running pod-shaped combs
through the strands
like she was unfurling gypsy fans.

After, you could still see
that hair reflecting shine
like the shine of enamel boxes
atop an antique table
on Mother's side of the bed.

Finally, she didn't waste any time
with me, sing or whistle;
briskly untangled, brushed, spit
down the nappy strays,
ten minutes tops.

Then out we all went,
happy and free,
if only for one summer
of innocent play,
Mother's lovely grand-girls
and me.

Composition #3

Whether born of a violence that cannot
call itself loving, of rats' nest or shadow
& piss, a child is meadow and psaltery,
is bird's wing, ginger, and lizard's eye.

Her birth is no one's malady, though some
are unwanted, rejected, or just traded for.
No one's less innocent than their mothers,
exiled to *I-chose-this-unpardonable-country*.

Light Curving Away from Earth

In an old photograph rescued
from a trash bin, Daddy stands
beside me, circa second grade.
A trapped space,
the circumference of lost chances
at conversation,
swells between us.
Tenderly, Daddy

tethers our Weimaraner
(straining at his collar)
quite close to his body. We all
stare at someone's operatic lens.
It's just past the vernal equinox.
The fall will come quite soon.

Siren

Eternally lured by calypso,
        Daddy wanted to return
                to his birthplace, to the Mighty Sparrow.

He knew about heat's seduction, about steel pans,
        maracas, about the Canboulay, all
                brewed in the Indies' crucible of revolution,

underpinning the peg box and scroll
        of a violin Daddy also favored—yes, Vivaldi!—
                who (his sons said) couldn't best Jellyroll

Morton and his hepcats blowing with the Nat King
        Cole Swingsters in every California beer joint
                until the money ran out; Sassy Vaughn singing

Black Coffee and *Nice Work If You Can Get It.*
        Daddy admitted Duke and Roach (with his *Jazz*
                in 3/4 Time) were superior to any minor minuet

but sometimes he had a hunger for a polonaise,
        a Schøenberg twelve-tone, a Bartók sonata that
                his daughter drowned out with Marvin Gaye's

Stubborn Kinda Fellow and Dizzy's latest platter.
        Still, Daddy reminded us to kiss the ground of Port
                o' Spain where stick fighting's clatter

gave way to fry pans and oil drums or
        anything that could shimmy up a rhythm and
                put a dip in the hip of a late-night worker

because that music had given birth to the flim-
        flam singers his children were calling musicians—
                men twisting their fingers so hard it seemed

they'd forgotten bamboo sticks, jawbones and
        Belafonte blowing into white America—*Day-O!*—
                and oh, we didn't have a clue about the Akan

or any other African tribe who handmade the first banjo,
        calabash, djembe, and the call of Zimbabwe's mbira,
                that siren luring Daddy back to his calypso.

Daddy Registered Republican, 1931,

but I learned about politics the year Mother called Mamie Eisenhower
a frump. "The papers can say whatever they want," she said, "but her
silly bangs and that stupid hat doesn't do it for me." (She said as she
crushed my shoulders between her knees, hot-combing my kinky school-
girl bangs.) "Didn't her husband have an affair during the war?" I took
it as a sign that Republicans should never live in the White House.

                        At first, Daddy, immersed in the copy
of *Life* magazine I'd seen him linger over more than once in the last six
months, didn't respond. On *Life*'s cover, a shot of the first Negro woman
ever to appear there—Dorothy Dandridge—one bronze shoulder exposed,
a red rose high-lighting her hair, a smile that made men. "I agree," was
Daddy's peculiar reply, "Dorothy is one god-damned fine-looking woman."

Domain: Los Angeles, 1959

He cut a figure, the stranger sitting
in our living room—a grey-suited

blue-tied nervous white man leaning
toward my Daddy while my Mother

leaned forward—never too far—
from the place she owned, concealed

behind the wall. "He's from City Hall"
she whispered, her face a reproduction

of English aplomb. "Yessir," City Hall
said, "L.A.'s going to build the I-10

freeway right though the molding of
your living room, but we'll make you

and yours a fine offer to move along…
I mean, to relocate." Daddy asked Hall

some questions I didn't understand but
the questions made blue-tie coil his lip

to hide his hostility and then he stood
just as suddenly as he had strolled in.

"Talk to your wife and family. Consider.
But make no mistake—the new highway

is coming through and you'll lose every-
thing." Just as gray-suit predicted, our

few options were *the* topic during dinner.
Daddy, who only raised his voice when

he knew he was right said, "his offer's just
another name for 40 acres in Mississippi."

White Flight: Los Angeles, 1961

The woman in the window is a dead ringer for
Donna Reed. Minutes ago, she sent her reasons
for living safely off: her husband with his flask

of milk, his Dragnet special; their daughter with
Heidi-hefty curls of gold; their sons perched atop
their Schwinns and armed with news about some

preacher named King; her man's *don't take chances*
drumming in her ears—*avoid the windows and lock
the doors.* Across the street, one of the neighbor's

boys (she can't tell them apart) re-mows the freshly-
mown lawn, transistor blaring Sam Cooke's *Chain
Gang* and surely no good can come of that. The boy's

father, his Caribbean-breeze-of-an-accent soft, leaves
earlier than her man, and that irks. On the telephone
wires above their houses, a flock of white-crowned

sparrows raise a squawk sensing the presence of a
blackbird, red hidden in its wings. *How do they know*
she asks later, *when it's time to fly?   By their sense,*

of imminent doom, her husband growls, spits, reading
about a sit-in at a southern Woolworth's, a version of
the 5-and-10 where his kids buy Coke and waxed lips.

Mrs. Wright

There was a woman who came to Sunday
cricket, one brother reported, who never
quite forgive Mother for not being white.

Believe it.

Mother's lips would twist like a curling iron
whenever we mentioned the woman's name.

Birthmark

no matter where we are living we will always be 3/5
Mississippi where memory is one long train whistle

Photograph: Aureola Boulevard, Easter, 1963

We're all there: my sisters-in-law in their Jackie Kennedy's;
our neighbor Janet from across the street whom we pray can
be brought to Jesus (although all I really want is her dark and

glossy ponytail hidden beneath a chapeau of *crêpe de chine*).
And yes, of course, my Mother, Queen Cluck, sporting gloves
of such elbow-length white they seem to promise: *everything*

is possible. Then me, on the end—all candy-stripped ribbons,
scarred knees, little hope; our virtues trapped by a Brownie.
Does anyone know what that means anymore? Do we rise?

The Curious Adoptee

I'd like to find her,
compare notes, ask

which of us got lucky?
I'd like to know

why? My parents
could have been

hers but something
fell through—as in

the rabbit hole,
as in *next in line,*

step up to somebody's
game or the funny papers.

Or, nothing fell.
God just said

"oops." He's only
God, after all.

When it was said
& done, I was in

so she was out;
out of luck

or lucky?

Lessons in Vernacular

If I was going to survive,
I had to learn to communicate.
Even Daddy agreed
but no slang, he frowned.

Still, I took lessons—in secret—
Friday nights—from a a girl who
was acceptable to the parents—
she was Episcopalian, after all.

Still, I never tried to practice my
new skills around the Heads-of-
Household. Never said *outta sight,
gimme some skin* or *lay it on me.*

It was a drag.

My Body Leaning Into

You might expect as centerpiece
West Indian Village With Figures

Dancing. Instead, my immigrant
parents buy a European imitation,

hang *Bal du Moulin de la Galette*
in our vestibule. All I can ask is

are these the women you both pray
I will be? It's impossible to tell where

each partner's shadow begins. Me? I
like Archibald Motley's *Saturday Night*

with its scarlet-clad heroine, her brown
arms unfolding from her body, her body

leaning into the rag & swing, one balding
man wishing he wasn't wishing, a shot of

bourbon & soda, bop & jive & jive & jive.
To stun Mother I say: *see the sommelier?—*

how far he's willing to back-bend, cock-
tails listing to such risky angles just so

he can wallow in the woman's satisfaction
in simply being the center of everything?

In 1968, My Parents Were Still Negroes—

even when Lyndon Baines signed the Civil
Rights Act, my parents were still Negroes
who would never mourn for Malcolm X
the way they would mourn for Doctor King.

They were still Negroes because despite My Lai,
their son was career military. Despite the Prague
Spring, they still watched *Wagon Train* and could
i.d. every has-been on *What's My Line?* In 1968,

a minor pop star, Frankie Lymon, overdosed—
heroin—but my parents were still Negroes in
love with Nat King Cole and NBC. While nerve
gas leaked near Skull Valley, did my folks know

people freed themselves in Mauritius? In Phong
Nhat, there was a massacre but Rowan & Martin
kept on laughin'. I graduated high school the year
Sirhan killed Bobby but my parents were still

Negroes when I left for college, knowing three
students were killed in an all-white bowling alley,
South Carolina. But *A Space Odyssey* premiered;
Hair debuted on Broadway & my parents, orthodox

Negroes, didn't get the Beatles or why students were
rioting in Paris. They were cheered by a Manchester
team winning the European Cup but remained mute
when Pope Paul VI condemned a little white pill.

My parents were still Negroes that August but watched
Chicago's convention in horror: Jerry Rubin, the Guard,
the Democrats and Daly—all the world reading his lips:
…you Jew sons of bitches…motherfuckers…go home!

Still, my parents were Negroes because they were no
longer niggers; because my Daddy drove a long, black
Cadillac and we lived on a cedar-lined street right next
to a white man from Georgia. White South Africans

excluded the Marylebone Cricket Club just as women
protested *Miss America*. When the Irish troubles got
worse and the 19th Olympiad cold-cocked Mexico City,
my parents didn't feel less Negro because John Carlos,

head bowed, raised his fist. But I did. The Rodney Riots
rocked Jamaica. The Queen of Soul won *Respect*. At Yale,
women enrolled and Miss Chisholm got the votes. In 1968,
my parents were still Negroes. They never would be again.

Religion & Crack

It wasn't like religion exactly—not
like when we returned from the Good
Shepard's sermon only to find Daddy
surrounded by the Latter Day Saints,
serving them Earl Grey & Bisquick
cake `til Mother gave them her heel.

Not like when they sent me to every
parochial school they could find: 7th
Day Adventist and two Lutherans (to
keep me on a straight and narrow street,
away from the boys and the "publics"),
then turning me on to Mary Baker Eddy
before Mother re-emerged Episcopalian.

But there was an element of the spiritual
in the way she spoke about the Dodgers
of 1959: Gil Hodges and Carl Furillo
playing at the Memorial Coliseum evenings
as she ironed Daddy's boxers to Vin Scully's
account of the Crack of the Bat of Moon.

How the Birth Mother Was Found

An old friend heard her laughing—
thought it was me because she'd

heard me laugh before. She turned to
the laughing woman. *I went to school*

with your daughter. The woman who
birthed me said: *I have no daughter.*

Bone-chip

She come lookin' for me—
oh, not directly but
she come—

knew anyone lookin'
at her   then
lookin' at me
would see   her   so

she polished the bones fixing
her head to her neck   turned
her wrist-bones to weapons

she practiced a dark hollow growl
she wanted to tumble from her throat
when she thought she should laugh

but she never laughed much   fell
unwell, yoked to life-long miseries
one who knew her told me later

said she had memories didn't know
how to forget their own placenta so
she come lookin' for me

put herself on a straight-away
bowed down low, jumped right
on up somebody saw   guessed

how wrong she'd been so she come
lookin'   found her daughter:
    ambivalent   chipped

the birth father

could have been anyone:
      a Pole
      a felon
      an identical twin

he could have been a Holy Roller
(although that seems unlikely)

he could have been
      an ocean
      a doorbell
      a slice of American cheese

he could have been
      goya—the Urdus'
      transporting suspension
      of disbelief

i suspect he was a train schedule
& every woman's intermittent

it's been my choice not to believe
      father once lived
      somewhere near
      Uncle Tom's cabin

or that, unbidden, Siri found him, said:
      your father is sitting beside me

What is logic in a hurricane's eye?

if he'd been my crossing guard, i could've adored him—
would have hated to know he never looked both ways

he has never been   but
       if you're of a certain age,
       he could have been yours...

Seam/stress

Every day that summer, Mother zigzagged &
lock-stitched in the room she kept for sewing.

Six *Seventeen* magazines atop a side table
and the *Singer* humming with the harmonics

of treble, footpad, bobbin; the indigo, yellow,
and scarlet threads threading it all; her scissors

in constant motion. I was off to college and
Mother made sure I would show up dressed

for the part. I'd never have to sacrifice the lucky
life she'd wanted. It's all there in Lindbloom's

Eagle, her high school yearbook, 1928: Spanish
Club & Honor Society & "have a fabulous time

at the University of Chicago" but Mother married
just after her graduation so her daughter wasn't

going to come up short. In the end, doesn't every-
thing come down to vanity, time? That summer,

Mother tacked and tatted skirts, shirts, slacks.
She stitched dozens of spools of fibers through

wools, corduroys, cottons, velvets for cool fall
evenings, until late in August, I was gone, heavy

luggage in tow. When I came home two months
later (torn jeans, no bra, hair wild as a funeral's

second line, unrecognizable) saying, *I haven't worn
any of it*, Mother wept, then sold her trusted *Singer*.

Red Background

It was the best conversation they ever had. The angry mother accused *that boy has a sex hold on you* giving the daughter all the ammunition she would ever need. The daughter told her mother that *she* had a sex hold on the boy—that in the end, she had given him revenge sex, remorse sex, that she had given it to him just because, or joyous *should I buy these shoes* sex? or *oh!—you have a new car* sex or *you wouldn't expect me to go to Verona and not have sex* sex, or sex for science as well as at the beach or in a gorge sex, sex in the kitchen before serving the cherries jubilee, red background sex in the style of Jean-Michel Basquiat and sex at 30,000 feet because *my what big hands you have—* O mommie, she squealed, the over, the under, the glory hallelujah sex!—the cemetery sex, the sex with a red light flashing, sex while she wore cotton panties & he wore only a tie. Ah yes, *that sex—*

Blush

Snatched from everything familiar, she quickly packed up her memories but a child's valise is small. Mother was born on an island rife with sweet fruit and that she never forgot. Once, in a market, I saw her seek out one ripe mango the way a bride skirmishes for her veil. When she found it, she cupped the fruit in her wrinkled palms as if it was a lover. It was greenish-yellow and blush of red and her body bangled its Carib bouquet. All at once, her eyes turned blue. In our kitchen, sitting apart, she relished the mango meat on her tongue as if it was religion. She let the juice run down her chin and throat and breasts. She did not look at us and, for a time all her own, she sat with hands closed, sticky with pulp.

Politics

Ironing taught me:
we are covered in white—

we are covered in white as white
as Dad's handkerchiefs, boxers.

Dad's handkerchiefs, boxers,
our pillowcases and bed-sheets,

ironing is what taught me.

*

Our pillowcases and bed-sheets
(when did I know of the Klan?)

What could I know of the Klan—
that lynchings were their norm?

In 1951, lynchings were the norm
and Harry T. Moore was killed

by pillowcases and bed-sheets.

*

Poor Harry T. Moore was killed
(He was a teacher, just like my Dad).

Moore taught school just like my Dad
who thought learning was the thing—

insisted learning was the thing
to make us more equal and free—

still, Harry T. Moore was killed.

*

Would we ever be equal and free?
Moore's murder is still unsolved.

Unsolved, his Christmas murder.
Ditto Hampton and Van Patter.

Hampton and Van Patter killed
and their risk?—to be a Panther,

to live equal, to live free.

*

But every panther takes a risk:
see: Watt's Riots, Daddy warned;

Daddy warned: *terrible these riots
where we burn our houses down.*

*When we burn our houses down,
ash is all that's left upon our hearts.*

Every panther takes her risks &

*

when we burnish black our hearts,
we leave artists to tell the stories,

the artists retell the stories like
John Outerbridge or Betye Saar—

John Outerbridge or Betye Saar—
check out his *No Time for Jivin'*

burning blackness in our hearts.

*

See his *No Time for Jivin;* see
her *Gris-Gris Box & Bittersweet,*

her *Gris-Gris Box & Bittersweet,*
my father's warning and my risk

despite that warning. I take the risk:
I burn a blackness in my heart.

This ain't *No Time for Jivin'*—

Erasure

The woman who gave me breath
erased my father, his whistle & pain.
She never said his eyes were brown.

She didn't remember how he moved
the night they made me. She omitted
details of geography and religion was

excised. Music never played or she
would have played it. She told me
my father's name. I can't repeat it.

In a Reflecting Glass—

…I am almost sure of what I see. Sure in the way I am unsure
about the time it takes to braise a young duck. It's something
over my shoulder that I'm seeing: black earth rising, breathing
like a sleeping child. Through my reverie comes a lake like glass,
ribboning along. I'd forgotten that a mirror can smell like lavender
or sometimes, putrefaction. Over my other shoulder, something else:
pinking shears, infinity, a pearl as cruel as a jewel. All these visions
exist at some distance and I love them—love being the favorite fickle
finger that makes me slightly nauseous so I focus on my forehead
where I see a forest of baobab older than forever, taller than my father
He, too, appears—inexplicably—in the mirror and I almost recognize
him. I almost forgive myself for that.

Thorn

Dear stinky-bottom, O could-have-been,
so-long-in-such-never-becoming, so dear
you could've been my split-from-a-round-
about. Instead, I have labeled you: *Thorn.*

Think of all that's been spared you:
the ferocity of me as mother, all civil
disobedience and swollen nipples,
using you to justify my (*select any*

neurosis and insert <u>here</u>), my finite
dis-ease hidden under a false veneer
of *trust me*; a flim-flam ma'am of the first
order saying *because I say so.* You are so

lucky, little-feet-tender-as-lambs'-skin,
gurgle-of-giggle, my little Trevi fountain.
Just think of the cruelty that was my
mother: shrunk-wrapped, set upon by

the curse of wanting, under the thumb
of The Great Thumb (*here read: auntie,*
priest, flu epidemic) and hardly a penny
to give thanks for. Deep shadow-under-

my-breast, be grateful wherever you are,
for wherever you are isn't as dark as
the miasma you would have lived in so
be glad, my Seed of Perpetual Dominion…

Relativity, a haunting

This is a confession of pedigree:
each brother drank blood and
sugar and grew great wings
from his hump-backed back.

Each brother chirped his singular
chirp: one crow, one lark; two
others, puffin and owl. Most days
they exchanged feathers, stymied

sharpshooters, flew under a radar
not yet invented, were husbands—
two of them, twice—to wives who
were not their kind: conch, garden,

grey matter, faun—curl of smoke
the two who got free. The brothers
loved differently, indifferently.
They hoped to live by the sea

but as it turns out, sea leaks.
Flight never took them far from
wrought gates. They didn't know
their mother until she turned

pillar-as-salt and let's not speak
of their father. They molted for
the shortest of long lives if you
believe in contradictory terms

and they lived to inflame purpose.
One careless rumor still haunts
a febrile clock: I'm their Sister-As-
Duckling. Is it my turn to take off?

Modus Operandi

Daddy's was a double kiss
motif—forehead, first, then
Mother's mouth   closed

No arms
but no shyness

No hand-holding
or love words

                    *

In an old sketch
(they are mid-life, casual)
her hair tumbles gray
his shirt gapes   unbuttoned
at its neck   They look
frankly at the artist
half-smile   all-knowing
less than a penny's-rim
of space
                    cleaving them

Patina

His wife doesn't sleep with him anymore.
He wavers, like candlelight—his chest

a rattling fer-de-lance. He calls *Dora Dora
Dora*—75 years old and he still dreams

about his mother all the long night long.
His wife's content on a sofa more restful

than any bed she's ever shared. She loves
the cool *I'll pretend these are queen-sized*

sheets; the way moon-glow slants its patina
at 1:42 a.m., loves how, *finally,* she is alone.

Their Shih Tzu barks his dreams of bones
because he is used to their arrangement.

Their unmarried daughter, who's asked to
come home, again, understands less than less.

Comes the dawn and the wife attends
to rote duties: her husband's breathing

apparatus in need of its regular click;
the dog scratching to be let outdoors.

Memento Mori

Daddy left us a box
made for tie tacks
that contained
no tie tacks
contained one yellow
screw driver
a government badge
one transistor tube
a light bulb
too small
to light anything
a pen knife
a pen
left us
as we are

The Viewing

One brother said "let's make it easy on ourselves
and bury her naked." But I couldn't, I wouldn't
dare do that to a woman who might return as haint.
I feared she'd return cursing, placing hot embers
on my head where she's still knocking around with
her orders, ominous warnings, and vague scent of
onions, a crooked thumb still pressed to my throat.

And yet, when we saw Mother last, she was laid out
in the finest final box we could afford, her mouth
pursed into a scarlet simper she would never have
simpered in life. Still, my brother's suggestion holds
a certain fascination. I think of it often. I can picture
the mourners who would have passed by her coffin
in a single, startled file, whispering "did you recall
that her hands were so small, her breasts so lovely?"

Cryptogram

She came back again last night
        in my dreams; she lounged

atop my library of scribbles.
        I don't know how

she got there, but while I wanted
        to speak of joy,

Mother only wanted
        to speak of collapse.

Neither of us said *love*:
        that burr & mystery.

She arrived without,
        unclothed,

salt in each hand,
        caught in the wrong.

My knees bent to
        an unnecessary apology,

an infinite sentence,
        no hyphen.

It was a long night:
        moonstone   and the rush of her.

Web

The mother of the mother who gave me
away was one of eleven born in Canada.

She unravels the tale as I watch my Grand-
mother's great-grandson study the hodge-

podge of a puzzle broken into innumerable
pieces. I consider him as he tries to decide

which piece will fit into which other piece
with just the right *click* so that he knows

the splinter has fallen into the place where
it belongs. I don't have the heart to tell him

his bulldog's eaten a generous corner of sky;
to point out the limbs of African treetops—

blue gum? kokerbooms?—at rest under a
sofa, intermixed with dust mites. I return

to Grandmother's unbroken spider-web of
memories: John Wesley, her grandfather,

oldest son of Elizabeth Ford and the African
she married, the African (given name: Hari

Orara), stolen from Madagascar, hawked to
Kentucky, run off to Pennsylvania, then on

to Canada (thanks be to the railroad running
underground) after he crossed a great lake.

The youngster squeals with delight—he has
noticed fragments of the blue gum's roots just

as Grandmother reveals the name tattooed
upon the African: *George Henry Thompson.*

Chord

for Beverly

I

She didn't ask for me
when she saw all of it ending
so I don't know how she went out.

Whether she wept or sang
Precious Lord or *I Wish I Knew*,
she didn't ask for me.

Perhaps she asked for nothing—
nothing being what she once chose.
I don't know how she went out—

whether dreaming of my father
or of the revulsion she had for her own,
she didn't ask for me.

She could have left one suggestion—
she didn't, and maybe she died hard.
I don't know how she went out.

Whether dreaming of me or furious
she was at the end of dreaming and
left with one last choice: not to ask.
I don't know how she went out &

II

I must tell you this: I did not go to her
before her breathing became shallow
so she never knew what I've become—

that, as another's daughter, I did long.
Still, dressed in apologies and alibis,
I did not go to her—

my feet stuck in the sludge
of my other mother's *don't do this to me.*
She never knew what I've become.

She never knew and no one's to blame.
Why can't every choice be just a choice?
Because I didn't go to her

and why not?—continually—and
even then, I didn't. What *is* that?
Even I don't know if I've become

a liar, always fire in the grate, or some-
one else's reason to be grateful but that's
not good enough. I did not go to her.
Anyone can see what I've become.

Haint & Haint

You've been dead for several years now:
      you've been several, mothers—
           you've been years.
           Dead
           for now—
           several nows.

Years, deadly mothers.
Several have been
your years—(several have been
           left for dead)—

Dead years—
      & I am several
      as you
           have been

                  even now.

Tambourine

I

I am a slaveship washed up on Spring
my name lost to history

I am joined to the tears of the crossing
a dwelling house yoked to the cane

I oscillate windward then leeward
ever pulled down and down

II

because memory lives beyond death (& I
saw one of my grandmothers—only once)

because my bones are carved from theirs
(from myth, frangipani, and stories, half-told)

because my name was never only my own
(and because I am that flying fish, that ghost)

III

you think you know me

The Mollusk Museum

I

Family

is and is not
a velveteen pillow

theater

a dinner hour mistake
with candied yams on the side

a box at the bottom of

flightless penguins
hitchhiking through town

footprints in a cemetery

II

Symmetry

two moon pies per gypsy

greedy art and dirigible need

rushes and reeds
tracing paper on papyrus

the solo, the ensemble

wood ticks
wax moths

hand-drum, thrum-
thrumming the hand

a river, a poplar
the same old questions

III

War

I come to struggle,
to eat the edges of;

to abrade the chemical
& the alchemical

in the falling night, always
a souvenir wrapped in a rigmarole;
Vivaldi versus Jay-Z.

I'm rapt in biblical passages but never
            in any Book of Revelations or
                        Koran or Green Hornet.

All is taboo. Every day is like any
other habit. A telegram never opened.

Who Giveth This Girl?

What has made and maimed me?
—Margo Jefferson

She took the name *Toy Cow*.

She was aware of her milk.

Re-naming > privilege.

At play = desire even when

day after year
she took the name she was given—

shredded it,
ate most,
sent the rest to church where the nuns are a little ballsy.

What's in a name
is a confoundment
is alkaline
is sky torn down like wallpaper.

Who giveth this name in wedded agony?

Sticks and claims
do not honor thy father so

Toy Cow is the name she took.

The boys called her _____.

The girls called her _____.

When she began,
she began to call herself.

Notes

The poems with this ornament beside their title were inspired by circumstances underlying the author's adoption.

"Composition #1"
    The italicized portion of the last line appears in Larry Levis' "Elegy With A Chimneysweep Falling Inside It"

"Terrible Fortune Inside My Head, Grenadine"
    St. Vincent & the Grenadines are islands in the Lesser Antilles, West Indies.

"Emigrations"
    The italicized quote appears in Deuteronomy 28:25, King James Bible.

"In 1930, Daddy Drove to California Without Benefit of 'The Negro Traveler's Green Book'"
    Section II of the poem is composed using lines from the *Green Book*.

"Emigré"
    EC is shorthand for Eastern Caribbean. "Googlies," "legbreaks," and "flippers" are types of pitches in the ball game of cricket.

"Fretwork"
    The title refers to architectural ornamentation found on homes in the Caribbean.

"Lost Spirits"
    Obeah refers to folk magic, sorcery and religious practices originating in West Africa. "Papa Bois" is a character in folklore who was a guardian of animals and trees. The "douen" are the lost souls of children who died before being baptized.

"Religion & Crack"

Mary Baker Eddy founded the Church of Christ, Scientist.

"Moon" refers to Wally Moon, an Los Angeles Dodger outfielder.

ACKNOWLEDGEMENTS

I would like to extend deepest gratitude and appreciation to Jane Hirshfield for selecting *Fretwork* for the Marsh Hawk Prize and for her kind words, and to Alison Saar for her generosity in providing the artwork for *Fretwork*'s cover; also to Dorothy Barresi and the Monday night crew: Candace Pearson, Carine Topal, Cathie Sandstrom, Mary Fitzpatrick, Brenda Yates, Judith Pacht, Marjorie Becker, Kate Hovey, Beth Ruscio, Keven Bellows, and Kim Young; finally, deepest gratitude and thanks to Susan Terris, David St. John, Patricia Smith, and Major Jackson for their unwavering support and guidance.

Thanks also to the Vermont Studio Center and the Napa Valley Writers Conference where many of these poems were first conceived, and to the City of Los Angeles for the Fellowship that supported the writing. Finally, love and honor to my parents, my brothers, and all my family—the blood and the nurturers—who are my best and most enduring champions and inspirations.

The author extends deep gratitude to the readers and editors of the following journals where these poems or versions of them previously appeared:

Affilia, A Journal of Women and Social Work / "Composition #1"

African American Review / "Bout for Jack & A West Indian Immigrant," "Émigré," "Photograph: Aureola Boulevard, Easter, 1963"

African Voices / "Daddy Registered Republican, 1931"

Askew / "Overnight Bag, Blue, With Broken Handle," "Tambourine"

Barrow Street / "Terrible Fortune Inside My Head, Grenadine"

C.O.L.A. 2016 Catalog / "In 1968, My Parents Were Still Negroes"

Crab Creek Review / "How the Birth Mother Was Found," "Thorn"

Cultural Weekly / "Hammer & Pick," "Lost Spirits," "White Flight, Los Angeles, 1961"

Ecotone / "Siren," "The Dresser," "Seam/stress"

Fifth Wednesday Journal / "Genesis," "Iron Horses & the Moon"

Foundry / "Chord"

Fourteen Hills / "Who Giveth This Girl?"

Fox Chase Review / "Patina"

In Posse Review / "Telling," "Wombsong"

Levure Literature / "Trace"

Louisiana Literature / "Mother Taught Me Ugly"

Luvina 57 / "The Viewing"

Margie (defunct) / "In America's Mirror"

Mentress Moon (defunct) / "Queens"

Moria Online / "Doomsday Haiku"

North American Review / "Red Background"

Ploughshares / "The Mollusk Museum"

Poetry Flash / Modus Operandi"

Poem, Memoir, Story (PMS) / "The Van Dyck"

Rattle / "Antilles, lesser," "The Curious Adoptee"

Room / "Carnival"

Solstice Literary Magazine / "Politics" (Winner, 2016 Stephen Dunn Poetry Prize)

Spillway / "Beverly Meets My Father," "Inter-mix'd," "Haint & Haint"

Tab, A Literary Journal / "While She Was Out Stealing, I Slept in Beverly's Womb," "Cryptogram"

Weave / "Blush"

Zocaló Public Square / "Birthmark," "Fretwork," "Virgil Avenue & Other Geographies"

The author is also grateful to editors of the following anthologies where some of these poems appeared: *Beyond the Lyric Moment; Coiled Serpent: Poets Arising From the Cultural Quakes & Shifts of Los Angeles; Resisting Arrest, Poems to Stretch the Sky;* and *Wide Awake: Poets of Los Angeles and Beyond*

About the Author

Lynne Thompson is the author of three chapbooks and the poetry collections *Start with a Small Guitar* and *Beg No Pardon*, winner of the Perugia Press Book Award and the Great Lakes Colleges Association's New Writers Award. She received Honorable Mention in Pushcart Prize XLII, an Artist Fellowship from the City of Los Angeles, and was a finalist for the 2018 Toi Derricotte/Cornelius Eady Chapbook Award. Thompson serves as Reviews & Essays Editor for the literary journal *Spillway*.

Thompson was born in Los Angeles, California, and received a B.A. from Scripps College and a J.D. from Southwestern Law School.

Jane Augustine *Arbor Vitae; Krazy: Visual Poems and Performance Scripts; Night Lights; A Woman's Guide to Mountain Climbing*

Tom Beckett *Dipstick (Diptych)*

Sigman Byrd *Under the Wanderer's Star*

Patricia Carlin *Original Green; Quantum Jitters; Second Nature*

Claudia Carlson *The Elephant House; My Chocolate Sarcophagus; Pocket Park*

Meredith Cole *Miniatures*

Jon Curley *Hybrid Moments; Scorch Marks*

Neil de la Flor *Almost Dorothy; An Elephant's Memory of Blizzards*

Chard deNiord *Sharp Golden Thorn*

Sharon Dolin *Serious Pink*

Steve Fellner *Blind Date with Cavafy; The Weary World Rejoices*

Thomas Fink *Selected Poems & Poetic Series; Joyride; Peace Conference; Clarity and Other Poems; After Taxes; Gossip: A Book of Poems*

Norman Finkelstein *Inside the Ghost Factory; Passing Over*

Edward Foster *The Beginning of Sorrows; Dire Straits; Mahrem: Things Men Should Do for Men; Sewing the Wind; What He Ought to Know*

Paolo Javier *The Feeling is Actual*

Burt Kimmelman *Abandoned Angel; Somehow*

Burt Kimmelman and Fred Caruso *The Pond at Cape May Point*

Basil King *The Spoken Word / The Painted Hand from Learning to Draw / A History; 77 Beasts: Basil King's Beastiary; Mirage*

Martha King *Imperfect Fit*

Phillip Lopate *At the End of the Day: Selected Poems and An Introductory Essay*

Mary Mackey *Breaking the Fever; The Jaguars That Prowl Our Dreams; Sugar Zone; Travelers With No Ticket Home*

Jason McCall *Dear Hero,*

Sandy McIntosh *A Hole In the Ocean: A Hamptons' Apprenticeship; The After-Death History of My Mother; Between Earth and Sky; Cemetery Chess: Selected and New Poems; Ernesta, in the Style of the Flamenco; Forty-Nine Guaranteed Ways to Escape Death; Obsessional: Poetry for Performance*

Stephen Paul Miller *Any Lie You Tell Will Be the Truth; The Bee Flies in May; Fort Dad; Skinny Eighth Avenue; There's Only One God and You're Not It*

Daniel Morris *Bryce Passage; Hit Play; If Not for the Courage*

Geoffrey O'Brien *The Blue Hill*

Sharon Olinka *The Good City*

Christina Olivares *No Map of the Earth Includes Stars*

Justin Petropoulos *Eminent Domain*

Paul Pines *Charlotte Songs; Divine Madness; Gathering Sparks; Last Call at the Tin Palace*

Jacquelyn Pope *Watermark*

George Quasha *Things Done for Themselves*

Karin Randolph *Either She Was*

Rochelle Ratner *Balancing Acts; Ben Casey Days; House and Home*

Michael Rerick *In Ways Impossible to Fold*

Corrine Robins *Facing It: New and Selected Poems; One Thousand Years; Today's Menu*

Eileen R. Tabios *The Connoisseur of Alleys; I Take Thee, English, for My Beloved; The Light Sang as It Left Your Eyes: Our Autobiography; Reproductions of the Empty Flagpole; Sun Stigmata; The Thorn Rosary: Selected Prose Poems and New (1998–2010)*

Eileen R. Tabios and j/j hastain *The Relational Elations of Orphaned Algebra*

Susan Terris *Ghost of Yesterday; Natural Defenses*

Lynne Thompson *Fretwork*

Madeline Tiger *Birds of Sorrow and Joy*

Tana Jean Welch *Latest Volcano*

Harriet Zinnes *Drawing on the Wall; Light Light or the Curvature of the Earth; New and Selected Poems; Weather is Whether; Whither Nonstopping*

YEAR	AUTHOR	MHP POETRY PRIZE TITLE	JUDGE
2004	Jacquelyn Pope	*Watermark*	Marie Ponsot
2005	Sigman Byrd	*Under the Wanderer's Star*	Gerald Stern
2006	Steve Fellner	*Blind Date with Cavafy*	Denise Duhamel
2007	Karin Randolph	*Either She Was*	David Shapiro
2008	Michael Rerick	*In Ways Impossible to Fold*	Thylias Moss
2009	Neil de la Flor	*Almost Dorothy*	Forrest Gander
2010	Justin Petropoulos	*Eminent Domain*	Anne Waldman
2011	Meredith Cole	*Miniatures*	Alicia Ostriker
2012	Jason McCall	*Dear Hero,*	Cornelius Eady
2013	Tom Beckett	*Dipstick (Diptych)*	Charles Bernstein
2014	Christina Olivares	*No Map of the Earth Includes Stars*	Brenda Hillman
2015	Tana Jean Welch	*Latest Volcano*	Stephanie Strickland
2016	Robert Gibb	*After*	Mark Doty
2017	Geoffrey O'Brien	*The Blue Hill*	Meena Alexander
2018	Lynne Thompson	*Fretwork*	Jane Hirshfield

ARTISTIC ADVISORY BOARD

Toi Derricotte, Denise Duhamel, Marilyn Hacker, Allan Kornblum (*in memorium*), Maria Mazzioti Gillan, Alicia Ostriker, Marie Ponsot, David Shapiro, Nathaniel Tarn, Anne Waldman, and John Yau.

For more information, please go to: **www.marshhawkpress.org**